ARTIST
TRANSCRIPTIONS®
SAXOPHONE

STAN GETZ

BOSSA NOVAS

Transcribed by Greg Fishman

ISBN 0-7935-8179-6

HAL•LEONARD®
CORPORATION

7777 W. BLUEMOUND RD. P.O. BOX 13819 MILWAUKEE, WI 53213

Visit Hal Leonard Online at
www.halleonard.com

Stan Getz

Stan Getz

Stan Getz was born in Philadelphia on February 2, 1927 and grew up in New York. At age 15 he received his first professional job with Jack Teagarden's band. He stayed with Teagarden for nine months and settled in Los Angeles when the band disbanded in 1943. He performed with Stan Kenton in 1944-45, Benny Goodman in 1945-46, and in 1947 he joined Woody Herman's band. In late December of 1948 he recorded his famous "Early Autumn" solo which launched his career practically overnight. He left Woody Herman in early 1949 and returned to New York to lead his own quartet.

Throughout the 1950s, Getz led groups introducing such personnel as Horace Silver, Al Haig, Tommy Potter, Jimmy Raney, Roy Haynes, Duke Jordan, Bob Brookmeyer, and Lou Levy. Even though the material he played consisted mostly of standards, some bebop tunes were also played. Getz was nicknamed "The Sound," and was widely known for his beautiful ballads. His solos during the early 1950s had an extremely introspective quality. "Yesterdays," from the album *The Complete Roost Sessions, Vol. 1* (Vogue VG 651), is a good example.

While critics labeled Getz "Cool," he was beyond categorization. Listen to the ferocity with which he plays "Parker 51" or "Move" from the *Storyville* sessions of 1952 (Mosaic MD3-131). Toward the end of the '50s, Getz's tone became much deeper, and the character of his playing acquired an earthy quality. "Blues For Mary Jane" from the album *The Steamer* (Verve MG-V 8294), depicts this quality.

Getz moved to Denmark in 1958 and recorded some excellent records (available on the Rarities label, from England) with bassist Oscar Pettiford. During Getz's absence from the American Jazz scene, however, Sonny Rollins and John Coltrane became the most popular tenor players.

Getz marked his return to the United States with a breathtaking album called *Focus* (Verve 821 982-2). The music, for strings and rhythm section, was written by Eddie Sauter; however, Getz's part was completely improvised. This was Getz's favorite record. Although *Focus* was a complete artistic success, it did not bring back the popularity he had enjoyed throughout the 1950s.

Upon the release of *Jazz Samba* (Verve V6-8432) in April of 1962, Getz's popularity once again soared. *Jazz Samba* entered the pop charts on September 15, 1962, reached the number one position, and stayed on the charts for 70 weeks! This album earned Getz a Grammy Award for Best Jazz Performance. In 1964, *Getz/Gilberto* (Verve V6-8545) reached number two on the pop chart, won eight

Grammy Awards, and gave the world "The Girl From Ipanema." The early to middle '60s were considered to be the Bossa Nova years. Getz was a natural for this sensuous, melodic, bittersweet music from Brazil, and his playing was marked by extremely inventive and subtle use of articulation and tonal shadings.

The commercial success of the bossa nova never dulled Getz's sense of creativity. In 1964, at the height of the Bossa Nova fad, Getz recorded a straight ahead jazz album with Bill Evans and Elvin Jones (Verve 833 802-2). Getz's working group during this time period performed both straight ahead jazz and bossa novas. This group, which included vibist Gary Burton, can be heard on the album *Getz Au Go Go,* (Verve 821 725-2).

By the middle 1960s, Getz formed yet another new group consisting of Chick Corea, Steve Swallow, and Roy Haynes. The album, *Sweet Rain* (Verve 815-054-2), is an excellent example of this group's musical interpretation. Interestingly, the night before the session, both Haynes and Swallow came down with the flu. On the morning of the recording session Getz hired Ron Carter and Grady Tate to play on the record. This record is regarded as one of Getz's best albums. Other

Photos by Ray Avery

groups during the late '60s included Jack DeJohnette, Richard Beirach, and Miroslav Vitous.

By the early 1970s, Getz's playing became more aggressive. By 1975 Getz's group consisted of Albert Dailey, Clint Houston, and Billy Hart. This explosive quartet can be heard, with Getz at the top of his form, on an album aptly titled, *The Master* (Columbia FC-38272). In 1976, pianist Joanne Brackeen became part of Getz's working group. The group can be heard on *Live at Montmartre, Vols. 1 & 2* (Steeplechase 8CCD-31073 & 31074).

Another World, (Columbia BL-35514) recorded in 1977, marked a new direction for Getz. This group included Andy Laverne, Mike Richmond, Billy Hart, and Efrain Toro. Differing from Getz's previous efforts, this was an electric group: electric bass, synthesizers, and even the occasional use of an Echoplex by Getz himself.

The 1980s was a decade of renaissance for Getz. He returned to an all acoustic quartet playing many of the standard tunes he had recorded in the 1950s. It's fascinating to hear how Getz's style changed when you compare standards, such as the 1952 and 1981 versions of "Body & Soul." The album *Pure Getz* (Concord CCD 4188) is a masterpiece. It features Jim McNeely, Marc Johnson, Victor Lewis, and Billy Hart. Selections include Bill Evan's beautiful waltz, "Very Early," as well as the Bud Powell classic, "Tempus Fugit."

Starting in 1986, Kenny Barron became Getz's new pianist. Getz's working band in the 1980s consisted of Kenny Barron, George Mraz or Rufus Reid, and Victor Lewis. The albums *Voyage*

(Blackhawk BKH 511-2), *Anniversary* (EmArcy 838 769-2), and *Serenity* (EmArcy 838 770-2), are excellent representations of this quartet.

In 1990, Getz collaborated with Herb Alpert and Eddie del Barrio in producing *Apasionado*. The album is similar to *Focus* in that Getz's part, for the majority of the album, was total improvisation supported by a large ensemble background. Getz shows again his uncanny ability to sound at home in any setting without sacrificing any of his own artistic qualities.

The last record that Getz recorded, *People Time*, (Verve 314 510 823-2) is a duet with Kenny Barron. It was recorded just three months before Getz's death due to cancer on June 6, 1991. While listening to the album, one can hear the pain, courage, love, and beauty that Stan Getz possessed.

An uncompromising artist, never content to rest on his laurels, Stan Getz was always searching and expanding his music. The following quote best describes Getz's musical genius: "My life is music - and in some vague, mysterious and subconscious way I have always been driven by a taut inner spring which has propelled me to almost compulsively reach for perfection in music, often, in fact, mostly at the expense of everything else in my life."

Greg Fishman

Discography

TUNE TITLE:	DATE RECORDED:	ALBUM TITLE:	LABEL & CATALOG # (ALBUM/CD):
Balanco No Samba (Street Dance)	August 28, 1962	Big Band Bossa Nova	Verve V6-8494/825 771-2
Chega de Saudade (No More Blues)	August 27, 1962	Big Band Bossa Nova	Verve V6-8494/825 771-2
Desafinado (1st Version)	February 13, 1962	Jazz Samba	Verve V-8432/314 521-413-2
Desafinado (2nd Version)	March 18, 1963	Getz/Gilberto	Verve V6-8545/314 521-414-2
Ebony Samba (Ist Version)	February 27, 1963	The Girl from Ipanema	Verve N/A /823 611-2
Ebony Samba (2nd Version)	February 9, 1963	Jazz Samba Encore!	Verve V6-8523/823 613-2
Entre Amigos (Sympathy between Friends)	August 28, 1962	Big Band Bossa Nova	Verve V6-8494/825 771-2
The Girl from Ipanema (Garôta de Ipanema)	March 18, 1963	Getz/Gilberto	Verve V6-8454/314 521-414-2
How Insensitive (Insensatez)	February 8, 1963	Jazz Samba Encore!	Verve V6-8523/823 613-2
Mania de Maria	February 9, 1963	Jazz Samba Encore!	Verve V6-8523/823 613-2
Melancolico	August 28, 1962	Big Band Bossa Nova	Verve V6-8494/825 771-2
Menina Flor	February 9, 1963	Jazz Samba Encore!	Verve V6-8523/823 613-2
One Note Samba (1st Version)	February 13, 1962	Jazz Samba	Verve V-8432/314 521-413-2
One Note Samba (2nd Version)	May 22, 1964	Getz Au Go Go	Verve V6-8600/821 725-2

TUNE TITLE:	DATE RECORDED:	ALBUM TITLE:	LABEL & CATALOG # (ALBUM/CD):
Only Trust Your Heart	May 22, 1964	Getz Au Go Go	Verve V6-8600/821 725-2
Quiet Nights of Quiet Stars (Corcovado) (1st Version)	March 21, 1963	Stan Getz with Laurindo	Verve V6-8865/823 149-2
Quiet Nights of Quiet Stars (Corcovado) (2nd Version)	March 19, 1963	Getz/Gilberto	Verve V6-8545/314 521-414-2
Samba de Duas Notas (Two Note Samba)	February 9, 1963	Jazz Samba Encore!	Verve V6-8523/823 613-2
Samba Dees Days	February 13, 1962	Jazz Samba	Verve V-8432/314 521-413-2
Sambalero	February 8, 1962	Jazz Samba Encore!	Verve V6-8523/823 613-2
So Danco Samba (Jazz 'N' Samba) (1st Version)	February 8, 1963	Jazz Samba Encore!	Verve V6-8523/823 613-2
So Danco Samba (Jazz 'N' Samba) (2nd Version)	March 18, 1963	Getz/Gilberto	Verve V6-8545/314 521-414-2
Vivo Sonhando	March 18, 1963	Getz/Gilberto	Verve V6-8545/314 521-414-2

Note:
All songs listed above are available in the Verve 4-disc box set: *Stan Getz - The Girl from Ipanema: The Bossa Nova Years*
Verve 823 611-2

A note from the author

The purpose of my first volume of Stan Getz transcriptions, published in 1993, was to present a general overview of Getz's entire career. The response to this book has been so great that I felt it necessary to transcribe at least two more volumes of his work. With an artist of Getz's stature, each stylistic period merits an in-depth study.

The second volume, *Standards*, featured many of Getz's classic solos from the 1950s. This, the third transcription book, focuses exclusively on Stan Getz's groundbreaking bossa nova recordings of the early to middle 1960s.

In collaboration with Charlie Byrd and great Brazilian musicians like Antonio Carlos Jobim, Joao & Astrud Gilberto, Luiz Bonfa, and Laurindo Almeida, Getz's bossa nova was both an artistic and commercial success. The music has such validity that it appeals to audiences far beyond the boundaries of the typical jazz listener. Although many imitators jumped on the bandwagon after Getz's initial success, none of them had the depth and authenticity of Getz's interpretations. Getz set a standard of excellence for the bossa nova that has yet to be equalled.

To fully benefit from this book, I urge students to repeatedly listen to each of the solos. Getz's mastery of the saxophone was never more in evidence than on the bossa nova recordings. Try to emulate Getz's use of articulation, dynamics, vibrato and tonal shading.

Repeated listening is important because it's the only way to internalize the many subtleties of this music that are impossible to notate. For example, how could one possibly notate the depth of emotion Getz extracts from a simple whole note?

Getz always played instinctively. In the middle 1980s, Getz was an Artist-In-Residence at Stanford University. Below, a quote from the liner notes of the Stan Getz CD *Voyage*, (Blackhawk BKH 511-2) gives us some insight into his musical philosophy.

"My area of the curriculum is *feelings*. When I was asked about my reaction regarding modes in a jazz theory class, I said: 'I don't care much for modes. It's <u>not</u> the <u>mode</u> that counts, it's the <u>mood</u>!!'"

Whether this music is new to you, or if you've spent your whole life enjoying it, as I have, you are about to embark on a great adventure that will bring you closer to the genius of Stan Getz. Enjoy!

Greg Fishman

TABLE OF EXPRESSIVE DEVICES:

Scoop:
Start pitch slightly
flat by lowering jaw,
then slide pitch in tune
by raising jaw.

Slur + Scoop (Ascending):
Slide into pitch of second
note by slowly releasing
finger(s) from first note.

Pitch Drop:
Slightly lower jaw to
drop pitch before
releasing the note.

Slur + Scoop (Descending):
Slide into pitch of second
note by lowering then raising
jaw.

Grace Note:
The grace note is to
be played as quickly
as possible so that it
takes no appreciable
value from the note which
follows.

Slur + Pitch Drop:
Gradually lower pitch of first
note by lowering jaw and
slowly depressing key(s)
for second note.

Grace Note + Scoop:
After releasing the grace
note, slide into pitch
from slightly below by
lowering, then raising
jaw.

Tied Unison with Scoop:
While sustaining note,
lower jaw and slide back
to original pitch in
the specified rhythm.

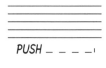

Push:
Play slightly ahead
of the beat.

Tied Unison with Vibrato Pulse:
Use vibrato on the note in
the specified rhythm.

Delay (or Lay Back):
Play slightly behind
the beat.

Half-Muffled Note:
Immediately after the initial
attack of the note, lightly rest
the tongue on the reed while
still sustaining the tone. Think
of pronouncing a letter "T"
immediately followed by pronouncing a letter "N".

SUGGESTED ALTERNATE FINGERINGS

T. = Octave Key

(Recorded on *BIG BAND BOSSA NOVA*)

BALANCO NO SAMBA
(STREET DANCE)

Bb TENOR SAX

By Gary McFarland

(Recorded on *BIG BAND BOSSA NOVA*)

CHEGA DE SAUDADE
(NO MORE BLUES)

Bb TENOR SAX

ORIGINAL TEXT BY VINICIUS DE MORAES
MUSIC BY ANTONIO CARLOS JOBIM

(Recorded on *JAZZ SAMBA*)

DESAFINADO

Bb TENOR SAX

Original Text by Newton Mendonca
Music by Antonio Carlos Jobim

FADE OUT

(Recorded on *GETZ/GILBERTO*)
DESAFINADO

Bb TENOR SAX

Original Text by Newton Mendonca
Music by Antonio Carlos Jobim

(Recorded on *JAZZ SAMBA ENCORE!*)

EBONY SAMBA
(SAMBANEGRO)

Bb TENOR SAX

Music by Luiz Bonfa
and Maria Toledo

(Recorded on *THE GIRL FROM IPANEMA, THE BOSSA NOVA YEARS*)

EBONY SAMBA
(SAMBANEGRO)

Bb TENOR SAX

MUSIC BY LUIZ BONFA
AND MARIA TOLEDO

(Recorded on BIG BAND BOSSA NOVA)

ENTRE AMIGO
(SYMPATHY BETWEEN FRIENDS)

Bb TENOR SAX

By Gary McFarland

(Recorded on *JAZZ SAMBA ENCORE!*)

HOW INSENSITIVE
(INSENSATEZ)

Bb TENOR SAX

Original Words by Vinicius de Moraes
English Words by Norman Gimbel
Music by Antonio Carlos Jobim

* FOR STUDY PURPOSES THE VOCAL IS NOTATED IN THE TENOR'S KEY.

(Recorded on *GETZ/GILBERTO*)

THE GIRL FROM IPANEMA
(GARÔTA DE IPANEMA)

Bb TENOR SAX

ENGLISH WORDS BY NORMAN GIMBEL
ORIGINAL WORDS BY VINICIUS DE MORAES
MUSIC BY ANTONIO CARLOS JOBIM

(Recorded on *JAZZ SAMBA ENCORE!*)
MANIA DE MARIA

Bb TENOR SAX

Words by Maria Toledo
Music by Luiz Bonfa

(Recorded on *JAZZ SAMBA ENCORE!*)
MENINA FLOR

Bb TENOR SAX

WORDS BY MARIA TOLEDO
MUSIC BY LUIZ BONFA

(Recorded on *BIG BAND BOSSA NOVA*)

MELANCOLICO

Bb TENOR SAX

By Gary McFarland

(Recorded on *GETZ AU GO GO*)

ONE NOTE SAMBA
(SAMBA DE UMA NOTA SO)

Bb TENOR SAX

ORIGINAL LYRICS BY NEWTON MENDONCA
ENGLISH LYRICS BY ANTONIO CARLOS JOBIM
MUSIC BY ANTONIO CARLOS JOBIM

* FOR STUDY PURPOSES THE VOCAL IS NOTATED IN THE TENOR'S KEY.

(Recorded on *JAZZ SAMBA*)

ONE NOTE SAMBA
(SAMBA DE UMA NOTA SO)

Bb TENOR SAX

Original Lyrics by Newton Mendonca
English Lyrics by Antonio Carlos Jobim
Music by Antonio Carlos Jobim

* KEEP HOLDING HIGH "E" KEY WHILE FINGERING "A".

(Recorded on *GETZ AU GO GO*)

ONLY TRUST YOUR HEART

Bb TENOR SAX

WORDS BY SAMMY CAHN
MUSIC BY BENNY CARTER

* FOR STUDY PURPOSES THE VOCAL IS NOTATED IN THE TENOR'S KEY.

(Recorded on *STAN GETZ w/LAURINDO ALMEIDA*)

QUIET NIGHTS OF QUIET STARS
(CORCOVADO)

Bb TENOR SAX

ENGLISH WORDS BY GENE LEES
ORIGINAL WORDS AND MUSIC BY ANTONIO CARLOS JOBIM

(Recorded on *GETZ/GILBERTO*)

QUIET NIGHTS OF QUIET STARS
(CORCOVADO)

Bb TENOR SAX

English Words by Gene Lees
Original Words and Music by Antonio Carlos Jobim

(Recorded on *JAZZ SAMBA ENCORE!*)

SAMBA DE DUAS NOTAS
(TWO NOTE SAMBA)

Bb TENOR SAX

Music by Luiz Bonfa
and Maria Toledo

(Recorded on *JAZZ SAMBA ENCORE!*)

SAMBALERO

Bb TENOR SAX

By Luiz Bonfa

(Recorded on *JAZZ SAMBA*)
SAMBA DEES DAYS

Bb TENOR SAX

By Charlie Byrd

84

(Recorded on *JAZZ SAMBA ENCORE!*)

SO DANCO SAMBA
(JAZZ 'N' SAMBA)
FROM THE FILM COPACABANA PALACE

Bb TENOR SAX

ORIGINAL TEXT BY VINICIUS DE MORAES
MUSIC BY ANTONIO CARLOS JOBIM

86

(Recorded on *GETZ/GILBERTO*)

SO DANCO SAMBA
(JAZZ 'N' SAMBA)
FROM THE FILM COPACABANA PALACE

Original Text by Vinicius De Moraes
Music by Antonio Carlos Jobim

Bb TENOR SAX

(Recorded on *GETZ/GILBERTO*)

VIVO SONHANDO
(DREAMER)

Bb TENOR SAX

Words and Music by
Antonio Carlos Jobim

About the author

Tenor saxophonist Greg Fishman is regarded as one of the foremost experts on the music of Stan Getz. An accomplished performer, recording artist and clinician, Greg Fishman is the author of three other books published by Hal Leonard: *Stan Getz, The Classic Jazz Master Series – Tenor Saxophone* and *Stan Getz Standards*.

Greg Fishman was born in Chicago in 1967 and is a graduate of DePaul University. He has studied with Joe Henderson, David Liebman, James Moody, Hal Galper, Mark Colby, Joe Daley, Alan Swain and Larry Combs.

He has performed with Louis Bellson, Clark Terry, Bobby Shew, The Woody Herman Band, Don Menza, Ira Sullivan, Eddie Higgins, Lou Levy, Ralph Burns and Conti Candoli. Greg is also the coleader of a jazz quartet which has toured the USA and Southeast Asia. He is the featured soloist on several recent CD releases.

Past awards include: First Place, 1992 North American Saxophone Alliance Competition; Second Place, 1991 Quest For Excellence Competition; First Place, 1985 Illinois Music Educator's Association.

Fishman's recorded work and live performances have received critical acclaim:

"Tenor saxophonist Greg Fishman nearly steals the show while sailing through Charlie Parker's '*Scrapple From The Apple.*' However, it soon becomes clear that boppish dexterity isn't his only strength, as he brings a warm, soulful, singing tone to several ballads that sometimes recalls the logic and lyricism of Stan Getz." - *The Washington Post* (review of Judy Roberts' CD *Circle of Friends*)

". . . highlighted by the exuberant cool tenor of Greg Fishman." - *Cadence* (CD review)

Photo by Glenn Kaupert

"Fishman, especially, outdid himself, creating brilliant solos in several extended works." - *Chicago Tribune* (review of Woody Herman Concert)

Of Fishman's first Getz transcription book, *Stan Getz, Saxophone Journal* says: "This book transcends a mere collection of solos. Included are a complete discography for all solos, a beautifully written Getz biography, and a to the point stylistic analysis of Getz' improvisational language and approach. Congratulations to Greg Fishman on his combination of scholarship and musicianship, and thanks to Hal Leonard for recognizing his efforts and including them in this beautifully packaged book."

THE MUSIC OF STAN GETZ

FROM HAL LEONARD CORPORATION

The legendary Stan Getz was one of the most creative and unique voices in jazz. These music collections let you play his arrangements, note-for-note.

STAN GETZ

Artist Transcriptions for Bb Tenor Saxophone

This carefully selected collection of 20 transcriptions includes famous Getz solos from 1948 to 1990. It also includes a biography and style analysis. Songs include: All the Things You Are • Body and Soul • Coba • Early Autumn • The Girl from Ipanema • Lover Man • Night and Day • Quiet Nights of Quiet Stars (Corcovado) • Yesterdays • and more.

00699375/$14.95

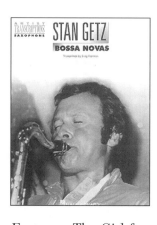

STAN GETZ BOSSA NOVAS

Artist Transcriptions for Bb Tenor Saxophone

18 solos exclusively from Stan Getz's bossa nova records of the 1960s. Features: The Girl from Ipanema • One Note Samba • Quiet Nights of Quiet Stars • Desafinado • Vivo Sonhando • How Insensitive • Only Trust Your Heart • Sambalero • Ebony Samba • and more.

00672377/$16.95

STAN GETZ STANDARDS

Artist Transcriptions for Bb Tenor Saxophone

This book focuses primarily on Stan Getz's ground-breaking recordings of standards from the 1950s. His recordings from this period hold a special place in the hearts of his fans. Includes a biography, discography, alternate fingering chart and table of expressive devices. Songs include: The Lady in Red • How Deep Is the Ocean • Moonlight in Vermont • Pennies from Heaven • Stella by Starlight • Thanks for the Memory • There Will Never Be Another You • The Way You Look Tonight • Willow Weep for Me • and more.

00672375/$17.95

FOR MORE INFORMATION, SEE YOUR LOCAL MUSIC DEALER, OR WRITE TO:

HAL•LEONARD® CORPORATION
7777 W. BLUEMOUND RD. P.O. BOX 13819 MILWAUKEE, WI 53213

Prices, contents, and availability subject to change without notice.
Some products may not be available outside the U.S.A.